A W E

WAVE BOOKS   SEATTLE   NEW YORK

DOROTHEA LASKY

AWE

Published by Wave Books

www.wavepoetry.com

Copyright © 2007 by Dorothea Lasky
Wave Books titles are distributed to the trade by
Consortium Book Sales and Distribution
Phone: 800-283-3572 / SAN 631-760X

Library of Congress Cataloging-in-Publication Data
Lasky, Dorothea, 1978—
    Awe / Dorothea Lasky. — 1st ed.
        p. cm.
    ISBN 978-1-933517-25-4 (limited edition hardcover : alk. paper) —
ISBN 978-1-933517-24-7 (trade pbk. : alk. paper)
    I. Title.
    PS3612.A858A94 2007
    811'.6—dc22
    2007012347

Designed and composed by Quemadura
Printed in the United States of America

9 8 7 6 5 4 3 2

Wave Books 012

There were countless generations that knew the story of Abraham by heart, word for word. How many did it make sleepless?

SØREN KIERKEGAARD, *Fear and Trembling*

CONTENTS

AWE

I knew that somehow in the midst of this confusion
Was the true dawning of myself.
My soul was a man and like a man
I would wander forever among the stars and flowers, lonely.
My heart a lonely star with no matching star
Anywhere in the universe and even so
Looking like a man for somewhere
To rest my freedom and resent it.

TOAST TO MY FRIEND OR WHY FRIENDSHIP IS THE BEST KIND OF LOVE

Laura, Laura I am sad for you
But more than you I am sad for me
And when I make a toast to you
I make a toast to me, my friend.
Here on the front porches of our lives,
I toast to you, with goblet raised.
And the house of our lives too, glittering
With decay. And the fatish ghost
Of losing and the sun and moon
Being the same thing outside our house, O!
That in decay we could find that losing
Is truly beautiful. I love you and what's so wrong
With that? Life is before us, so let us live!
In friendship we are one together and in friendship
I am all soul. No that's wrong, too.
What is a soul all aflame?
If it's a bird in snow,
Then that's what I am.

THE PROCESS OF EXPLICATION

I

Students, look at this table
And now when you see a man six feet tall
You can call him a fathom.

Likewise, students when yes and you do that and other stuff
Likewise too the shoe falls upon the sun
And the alphabet is full of blood
And when you knock upon a sentence in the
Process of explication you are going to need a lot of rags

Likewise, hello and goodbye.

I I

Nick Algiers is my student
And he sits there in a heap in front of me thinking of suicide
And so, I am the one in front of him
And I dance around him in a circle and light him on fire
And with his face on fire, I am suddenly ashamed.

Likewise the distance between us then
Is the knife that is not marriage.

III

Students, I can't lie, I'd rather be doing something else, I guess
Like making love or writing a poem
Or drinking wine on a tropical island
With a handsome boy who wants to hold me all night.

I can't lie that dreams are ridiculous.
And in dreaming myself upon the moon
I have made the moon my home and no one
Can ever get to me to hit me or kiss my lips.

And as my bridegroom comes and takes me away from you
You all ask me what is wrong and I say it is
That I will never win.

He was always distant.
No he wasn't

Yes he was, you told everyone.
Sometimes he wasn't

And what about poetry?
My friend said she wanted to kill herself because she couldn't write a poem

Well, what's it to you?
I understand, I want to kill myself now

And what about the real one over there. He loves you.
He never calls

Yes he does, when he can.
Not really, not with the obsessive quality he should

I love him.
Why?

He's sweet. He reminds me of the forest.
Of the fog on the forest in California?

No, not that, the other sort of forest
With the fires and that sort of thing?

Yes.
No, not like that, like the fog.

And what is the fog?
I don't know, the world's saliva

Do you really mean that?
Yes I do, I mean the spirit

And what about the things you've learned?
They mean nothing

And fire?
Nothing

And what of longing and the din of metal?
Those are occupiers. Leave me, I am free.

Then why are you still awake?
Freedom is not contentment. Freedom is only art.

And is love art?
No, art is nothing like fire

And how do you feel?
I am burning

And what is happening?
My spirit is ascending, my soul is trapped

And what is trapping it?
God. God and Awe.

THE DODO BIRD

[RAPHUS CUCULLATUS]

Some have described
The dodo's beak as actually grotesque.

It was long, pale yellow, and crooked.
But what other thing is like that? The sun!

And the sun upon my winglets
Has made me something no other bird or sun can compare.

And in meditating myself upon the bird
I have found that I could actually love.

My love, what are you that the dodo isn't?
Economy, the black mark on the sun,

The childless watch over the heavens?
Or is the dodo the thing growing from the sun spoke?

Yes, yes, that is you.

WHATEVER YOU PAID FOR THAT SWEATER, IT WAS WORTH IT

Be scared of yourself
The real self
Is very scary.
It is a man
But more importantly
The man is tall
And is everything in you that is an absolute reverse of all your actions.
In you he will do things and in you no one will know the difference
Still the honey and the herb, the bright lights.

The piece of fiscal fish, the lemons,
The blank above with stars will praise you
But he, he puts his legs over frail women
And tries to get to the thing they won't give up.
Just as true loneliness gets to the very real thing in you
Scary or not, is part man for all it is wanting and can't get
To the place where it has married woman, it sits
In a sea of lemons, its tail dragged bloody across the floor.

Still, here I do not speak of mutilation.
The real self is not muddy, it is pure
Still here it is a thing of murder
The self comes off itself and murders the woman in its path
Her skirts effortlessly careening back there up into the stars.

Weeks and weeks stretched out of the 18-year-old's brain.
The cold air whipped against the window and crawled at the windowsill.
Two weeks ago she had broken up with her
30-year-old loser boyfriend and now she lived
With her mother, who was paper thin.
And her mother was not nice either. She locked herself
In her room and when she did come out in
Her nightgown to ask for something, she
Barked at the 18-year-old.
On one such time, the 18-year-old got frustrated
And emptied out into the cold street.
Outside her door was a black man
She had once slept with. A lemon tree was
Growing ever so slightly from his forehead.
"Stop with these surrealistic tendencies!" he said
And pushed her away and she kept walking
To the house where her loser boyfriend was
Staying and knocked, but the neighbor lady told her
That he must be in a coma. She rattled at the door chains
And screamed. From the inside she could see
He was waving and holding up a sign that said
NOT NOW! in capital letters. The letters were red.
Her face ached and a light symphony played from the sky.
Being an 18-year-old she didn't ask too many questions, and went on,
And eventually she called her friend on her cell phone

And they decided to meet at the 7-eleven
In 10 minutes. 10 minutes came and went and
Soon they were together, sitting outside of it,
Drinking soda, and staring at the horizon.
Her friend told her that honesty was the best and that
Order was the best and that a self-ordered honesty
Was what to strive for and that an honest order
Was beautiful like a winter sky in Asia and
She did not believe this, she couldn't.
She did not believe anything honest was good.
Since the world had been so dishonest with her,
She would veil herself in lies, until
She was shrouded in a thick, dark cocoon.
She didn't say anything in response to her friend
Except the utterances we emit when we are truly listening,
And she stretched her arms out in a great despair and walked on.

PHILOSOPHIES

The man who murders his wife
Is not the same as the man
Who goes around and murders a stranger.

I am a woman but I am not
The same as another woman.
Identity politics are bullshit.

There is only the smart and the evil,
The good and the righteous.
There is only one color on the earth.

In its infinite degradations it becomes music and mathematics.
There is shit on my hands
When I have been playing around with specifics.

Love your lover. You are a lover.
With each breath God has put a golden faith
Upon the snowy mountains of the world.

Here, look at the snowy mountains,
Glittering with snow.
They are wiser than you might think.

And in your soul, the small grey animals
Of the world sit and wait to do good
For you, and together

We are one thing, bleating a
Somber, scurrying lullaby to
Lapsing pinkish angels.

Upon a mountain
The angels smile sleepily as they stretch
Their very long legs, thinking of us.

And wise they might seem, us and the angels,
But really it is only God who is wise.

EMOTIONS

The flat balloon
Wraps around the child's face.

This is how it feels when you talk to me,
I can't get out of it and you say very little.

My hands are holding
The balloon tightly on the child's face.

I want the child to feel life.
I want to feel

The pain that the clouds have made for me.
Suddenly the child springs up, gets me a present, and says thank you.

His dog follows after him
And the dog is made of snow and so am I.

They sat in the Chinese restaurant
With the sun lit outside, but there was no sun in there.

There was a green scorpion to the right of her on the wall.
A gold plant did not bloom on the baseboard.

The people came out with plates of meat and rice
And she gingerly fed her friend with her fingers.

They both had gotten the same letter the other day.
One with gold writing from the 14th century.

It told of a man with many properties
And these things were for them now.

"Shall we buy a truck?" she asked and her friend stared blankly.

His eyes completely like the sky and in him
Silent bugs that are even silent with themselves.

He took her hand and they slow danced
Over the baseboards, careful not to hit the empty tables.

The people clapped, everyone around them was good
And they had cut flowers for such a love.

The flowers scattered themselves everywhere
And then crawled and scurried into wreaths.

He took two wreaths and put them on their heads.
And an old king came out from the wall and blessed them.

And the cook came out from the kitchen and splashed them with holy water.

And the cook took out two syringes and did a medical procedure.
And their blood was swapped with rosewater.

And sweetly they laid down in front of everyone on a golden bed.

Kissing and caressing the bodies they once hid from themselves.

Then the thief came in and stole their bodies forever,
But of course their spirits are still there

Playing hide and seek under the tables, and that sort of thing.

ANOREXIA

A bird is flying above a forest. I could say he was a blackhawk but what's the difference? There is nothing living in the forest. Except the trees are there and the mudwort, but nothing is living like the bird. The bird is flying above the forest. One wing is bent. He is trying to make sense of the hole in his chest. *Holey Moley* he says spinning around the forest, and the trees and the wuddleflowers spin around, *Holey Moley* they say and laugh with him.

MANIA

I am in a blue sea and I am wearing a red nightie. The nightie has been ripped in places most of all by the nighttime. This sea is made of girdle-doves and thing-a-ma-bobs. O yes and Bob too. Bob is kissing me and giving me flowers. He is giving me 8 headaches with his spinning finger. The finger he has made to court me but he does not realize no man who lives shall court me or please me. It is God who pleases me with his high and mighty and his amen and the room stretched out in light like a thin muscle flayed into the sun.

INSOMNIA

The young thing wrapped the fruit in sequins and showed it to the nun. The nun said good day and got it a goldfish. She got it a goldfish and special gloves to handle herself and the fish. The night is always full of surprises, I tell them now. The moonflowers had been dyed black in hell and the nun and the thing knew it. They both knew the thing would one day murder the nun, its thick fingers coiling and wrapping tightly around the nun's neck.

DEPRESSION

The stars are made of yellow paper but I did not know this for a long time so I wandered a marshy place looking for The Green Leprechaun. The Leprechaun and I were good friends even though he was a Capricorn and wore strangely pungent gloves. We ate dinner together on Tuesdays and Wednesdays and after dinner I'd curl his hair and give him lemon drops. I'd slide the drops down his big throat like good old Aunt Lolly used to do to me and give him a bath in Kahlua.

OBSESSIVE COMPULSIVE DISORDER

The murder took place on a day that was made for the children. He took the children and mashed them into a bucket. He made us eat it. I had to eat it! Afterwards he smelled his fingers so we smelled our fingers. Our hands stunk but actually quite sweetly. We all wore matching socks that were green and tan. The green was a nice green like the green an apple makes in the summer heat.

PARANOIA

I fell in love once with a train conductor. He used to oil the trains with his urine and belch on himself. We would go places with his parents and they would belch too. No I wasn't surprised. My wits were always about me. I stayed demure like a demon, quietly reapplying my lipstick on the hour and half-hour. My lipstick was called Ancient Brick but really it was more of a mauve. Right before the love affair ended his mother and I would sneak in the bathroom together and change stockings.

AUTISM

A singer was trying to remember her songs but all she could think of was socks. *O Pasiphaë, my Great Mother* she would cry *What has happened to my sight?* bumping around her tower like a blindball henchman. The tower stretched up forever into the heavens. 10 feet above her some crows perched and circled, then perched and circled. *Farewell* she sang and no one was listening.

ALZHEIMER'S

I am made of lead, mushrooms, and rice. I am sitting here eating my blood (and yours too!) Come with me we will drink blood and brain! Come with me we will drink blood, brine, and brain! We are all children here made of folds and staples. We are made of folks that don't know we are listening. The ocean is floating above us like a quiet ring of moon. There is a ring of men here dancing around the moon throwing napkins at us.

PANIC ATTACKS

In a dream I had a heart attack and forgot how to breathe. Then the dream followed me to my real life and no one would have sex with me. Not even the people I asked nicely. In the shower I would shake and shake. In the shower my husband would come in and try to have sex with me, but I did not want his dick. I wanted a row of dicks all filled to their tips with oxygen. I went from shower to bed, to shower to bed, never really getting anywhere.

SCHIZOPHRENIA

A bunny came to my room and gave me a wish. He was actually part bunny and part man. He had waited for a new head but no one could find him one. His head was enormously large. He had walked into my room and smarted his head on the ceiling. *I am all head* I said and showed him I had no legs. He smiled and rubbed my tummy with a smooth washcloth and then a coarse one. There was nothing new in the world there at that moment and I assure you there is nothing new now either.

POEM FOR MY BEST FRIEND

Laura Solomon you are my best friend.
Outside the house where I grew up,
If you turn the outside lights off,
There is a nightglow one could only claim as eternity.
In the imperfect way that
All humans are perfect
You are perfect and guess what else is perfect?
All of life.
When you are loved, life fills in you
And there is reason for us all.
Now there is something between me and
The boy from the other side.
There is something between me and him
And his gleaming teeth on mine
Fills me with the wonder life cannot take from me.
O that I am nurtured at the sight and taste of love!
O that the moon and the big tree
Of my childhood glow on me
With metered abandon and you must know it too
Being that we are both poets
What glows on me, glows on you.
And if that be love,
Well then all the better.
And the generosity from my heart
Will fill your own with metered music.

And if both our hearts swell with the love I feel
From his sweet hand on mine
Well then all the better, too.
Bird in snow and love mouth wet with rain
And hands full of rain
The mouth of rain leaving us
And filling up the world
With a love the world cannot make itself.
And if that is not enough reason for us
Then whatever is is something I am never meant to understand.
And in not understanding, I catch the bird.
And the bird, shaking and silent
Gurgles in my hand, brown and bleating, and
Slowly he fades away.
And in empty palm the moonglow
Shines on me and my right hand
Becomes the mirror of the world
And my left, the black sunset.

The fire of the poem is within this bird.
O Lord poem!
My Lord poem, serva me.
Save me O Lord from men, who are sure to poison me.
Save me from abuse and wisdom and red hot sin.
Take me into the pure fire, the red eye
The burning fires of morning
That impinge their soul in winged flame.
And on the flame of my tongue
O that Lord, it was I, burnt out more holy than the rest.
O that I on winged flight
Reach into myself and pull out
The pure gold baby that
Burns to a shriek.
In the sun we will all come clean
And washed of our bones
The finger of light, the translucent devil
He makes his soft bed amongst our bones.
And on our bones, he lays his devilish tongue
Licking the marrow of you Lord from us.
And O that I were pure enough
To melt among the earth and trees
And be one with the woods!

The heart of me, bursting within itself!
Like a tree burst of its brain.
And flying above in golden ash and talking tree-like in fiery breath.
It would be I dissipating with you my Lord
In almighty fiery word.

They have peaches, plums, cherries,
Dewberries, and bananas there on the trees.
My mother used to put the fruit in jars
To last us all winter.
Nowadays the young people they buy
A can of fruit at the store and do not
Grow their own food. My mother used to
Pick the fruit off from the trees and
There were peaches, plums, strawberries,
And blueberries and in a jar they would all go and
Feed us all winter. Today the young people they
Buy a can of green beans and then they eat it.
It used to be that the fruit was on the trees there
Right back in the woods.
The fruit we picked off so easily, like talking
I would pick the fruit off the trees and give it to you.
The peach I would take off before mother canned it.
And the juice would drip down to your chest
And I would lick it off. Nowadays the young people
They have no children, they eat canned pineapple
Their mouths spilling out with nails and their intestines, they
Fall dry and brittle in their houses.
In my mouth though I will hold you
Even though they all have they all have forgotten
The sweetness of peaches and today

The children eat glass peaches and they try to remember
Something they can't even remember
Because it never even happened to them.
And that is sad, don't you think?
Don't you think that is sad? That here
We all are and we have all dried out.

THE MOUTH OF THE UNIVERSE
IS SCREAMING NOW IN AGONY

If Travis meets Monica but does not like Monica
then what's the use? There is no use in love
without purpose. There is a bluebird in
the purple evening sky. He is not the blackbird,
bleeding jagged red and the trees are blue.
There is silence among birds, and I have
need for silence. There is a noise in my heart
and I think it's my spirit. For instance it is the
spirithead that clangs. The children of
this world run past me. There are black
trees everywhere, with puffy round leaves
and the leaves are black. I have met me
but what's the difference. I am not
Travis or Monica and I do not love. It
is me who loves black earth and red sky,
the sun gold and the music sweet. You are
me too and you and I together sit on the earth
with the black trees high above us, everywhere a
hint of green. The green music of the
earth is the spirithead of the earth and from
the spiritmouth we spit and from our spiriteyes
we blink. The sun is hotter in our
minds than the situation. The spiritsun
is noisy with light. The blackbirds are

in orbit around its yellow body
like a burned-out picturescreen and when
we love it is us who breaks free, our
blackened bodies the nightsky to the
sleeping bodies in love, twisted and warm
and orbiting themselves around a paler sun.

NEVER SO IN LOVE

Laura was never so in love with Scott
Until they broke up.

She told me how after they broke up, how in love they were.

And how they enjoyed each other's company
At dinner once again.

And how over two pizzas they marveled
At the ecstasy of their conjoined thoughts.

And how later when they made love
It was the best love making ever.

And oh the tingle of the touch of Scott.

Laura, I said, I have never been so in love
With anyone until this moment

As I am in love with my first love Jason
Who in a small house in St. Louis

Tends to a baby he made with his wife Margaret.

My dog Lucy too is not so she has never been

So in love with anyone

Until this moment the rat
Has slipped from her mouth's grasp.

God too

Has never been so in love with the sun
As in this moment

He let go the sun
For us all to see.

Somewhere there are small children wading in a pool in the summer sun.
They have yet to know what love is.

PORTRAIT OF ME AND
VLADIMIR MAYAKOVSKY

Possibly all we have is chemistry
Perhaps it is chemistry that
All we have, this said, the fat man.
It is fire that turns the word.
God has only to turn a letter
To make one word another word
In Russian, God only has to turn
One letter to turn towers into
pastures. What the cold star of pastures!
In Russian, it is I God
In the Russian, the horses here are burning
That God may speak to us, it is towers
We too must take, that we
Refers to the star-infested,
That the cold-star bane is a huge ear.
That the soft flesh is a huge and horrible
Lady, yes, you Vladimir
And we too in the kitchen we too
The stars too, in horrible black trousers
We sit together at light, its huge ear
At tea cookies and violet and the stench of sweet
It is sweet that is the seed.
We sit at tables, it is Russian
That gives us the wood and the seed

It is tables that we sit
In the Agent District of the Third Moscow
A great cat, the provocateur.
And the Alluder, lit where
Mayakovsky lived. It is I
In the light we clink
Together the Tsarist with coffee
It is across the bodies that we eat meat.
It is across the bodies of the stars
You, Vladimir Mayakovsky, and I
Bend down to kiss you, milk aching
From my breasts, and the chrysanthemums of the age
A chemical unlike space here or time
It is you, with gargantuan lips and me
In tribal lip that we here too the stars do speak.

THE RED ROSE GIRLS

I

The Red Rose Girls were unlikely girls
H.D. liked them anyway and they spent their time in the insides,
    growing soft.
Inside they were all mush, and roses rotting
And when people spoke to them their
Insides wilted from the inside
And not from the outside, which as it was,
Was bright and blue and plastic.

II

There was a time the Red Rose Girls went into death
And death was untuned to them and he made them an unlikely hole
To hide themselves from anything
And the place they hid was mathematics and really was nothing
And also was its lesser art, astrology
Which of course is everything
And in math and astrology their heads burst out of the dragon
Like an unlikely pair
Of dragons, one with half a leg and
The other, untuned and slightly bumpy.

III

The Red Rose Girls went out to
Sit on the beach and Woolf was there, her arms outstretched
And into them they went, she was their lost daughter
And kissing her arms extensively
She was bat-like and her arms outstretched
A great many oceans and they were all sisters, kissing the arms
Of a great eternity, too large to even be
Compared to things that are small.
And the picture they have of that day is on the dresser.

IV

The Red Rose Girls told the day anything
For there is nothing the day
Can't handle, its bright smart being
The way hell out of war and marriage
They got their way out of war and marriage, those devilish leopards
Cancering and in them
The folds of the great bat,
Unlikely and mean.

V

I am finally in The Red Rose Girls, and mean
I mean to say
I am in the girls and mean and can't get out
The place of me not mean and unstartled
And unlikely to be the rose all bunched up
In it its core is a universe of cats
And inside the universe is the scary sound of cats
Their heartbeats and hoofbeats making a universal mistake.

V I

We the Red Rose Girls have made
A serious mistake, the universe is unlikely
Our hearts are sore, the roses
Our heads are folding over like the bat's, with wings outstretched
And in the brain is a wing
And unlikely that, a graph
Of Europe and the grizzly arts
Made by the machine men.
Their little metal hearts,
Elephant-like and supple.

It has come to my attention that your soul is in need of saving. Well, with all of your vice and your scorn. You spend a lot of time doing bad things, don't you? You might be asking yourself: How can I get into heaven? The truth is, there is no way. There is no heaven. The answer to Man's most asked question therefore has no answer. Let me tell you a story.

There was an elephant once named Jesus. He was full of blood. There was blood on his face and on his head, and on his body. His grey body would get all bloody and then get even more grey with all the dried blood. His skin felt like wet parchment, and I'll tell you a secret, I knew a little girl who would draw on him. Then Death came and killed the little girl and the elephant.

Friend, did that make little sense? Let me tell you something else. The Bible says "The Wages of Sin is Death" (Romans 6:23) and William Blake says "A Spirit and a Vision are not . . . a cloudy vapour, or a nothing" (*A Descriptive Catalogue*, 1809). Your spirit is in danger, sinner! You do not know your body is your spirit! The spirit on your tongue is full of water! The ball of fire in the sky is your heart on fire in your chest!

Friend, we are entering an apocalypse. That apocalypse is called *Lack of Divine Image*. This apocalypse has crushed our very general heart and is in danger of crushing our very specific one.

You might ask: what can I do? Well, here's what. Take the exit Nothingness 75 off the freeway. Give into yourself and oppress the law. Art is in danger, my brother and sister and sadly, you are in danger with it.

There is a rose for dividing water. Divide the water. Deeply concern yourself with this or the effect will be circular. Take the rose and put it in your chest, then put your chest in the sun. I'm serious. Without your help, no one will be saved. There will be no water. The earth is dying as we speak. So start now. God waits for no one.

Signed,
The Eternal Damned

ON OLD IDEAS

Kissing the bankteller outside his stairs
In Brighton, MA I cannot lie, I felt the hope
That we once felt, if only for an instant
O the lovely bankteller, like a moose he
Rode my spirit quite outside my clothes
And chrysanthemums sprouted I assure you
Out my nipples when he kissed them.
And the pureness of not knowing him at all
Was really what we all feel when we enter this earth.
There is a newness to the best things that cannot
Be excelled and old things like old love die and rot.
There are old ideas in the world that should be forgotten
There are old ideas and old phrases that should at least
Be recycled for others
There are old plans now that should be new.
There are old thoughts in your head, my reader, and let them die.
Follow me, I am the crusader of the new
My spirit is a plastic rod that channels all our births.
And in the mouths of the little beasts, we shall find the great
Ocean that spits up black bugs all glittering on its shores.
You know there is an anthem to the ages.
There is an anthem of the ages.
This is that anthem
This is that anthem

JOHN ALBERTSON IN THE SUMMER SUN

O John Albertson, you are so summery
In the summer sun.

You are so summery

You summery summery love.

You sunny summery kiss on the forehead and cheek.

Kiss me on the forehead and cheek, then kiss me on the lips.

Kiss me on the lips and hold my breasts.

Hold my thighs and breasts and then hold my breasts.

Hold my thighs to your thighs, then take me inside of you.

Hold me in your stomach and make a baby out of me.

I think it is sweet that you have a cat.

I think it is nice that you have a cat and call
It Mr. Fingers.

When we talk on the phone, I want to say:
"Well hello Mr. Fingers." And the cat would say back

"Well hello."

DIABETIC COMA

I got a brazilian wax for my engagement
But my old man was in a diabetic coma.
"Sweet Death!" he cried and I gave him a shove.
"Now this is the truth" we all thought
As he lay there, feeling nothing.
We pricked him and he whimpered a little,
But really nothing.
Four elusive spiders went crawling on him
But he had no human instinct
To grab at the elusivity.
I got my back-up dancers and we tempted
Him with the sin of women,
But his sugar level was so rich he couldn't see.
So we slipped him under the ground
And let the bugs eat him
Since that's what he really wanted anyway.

In your mouth the soul gapes out.
The dogs gape out.
The men eat grapes.

In your rib, a bird looks out.
The bird is an airbird.
Scratch its head. It is holy.

In your head is the smallest lion that has ever lived.
Take it out and give it air. It is dark and damp in your head.
Your brain eats away at the lion.

Outside your body is a set of bleachers.
Look across them, but don't look at the people.
Trick the men to do sleeping, caress the feet of the women.

For the women are the bodies that will make you come into being.
You will not know this for a long time.
You will sit stupidly and drink milk.

THE SIGN ELEMENT AND THE
ABILITY OF THE SPEECH ANIMAL

A poem is like a sparkly ring,
It must be glittering at different points as the light hits it.
The great vision of art is one of simultaneity.
So that there are many arcanes of the divine
Available to the readers of poetry at one time.
So says you and you know nothing.
Except to race to the footbath
With your little red cheeks.

And still the management of the divine
Is somehow meant like music.

We brush the grass of the earth
And weep at the heart of our feet.

Vacant here our cheeks are vacant
With the fullness of language.

Surrounding the fatness of our tongues
So that the fat letters of the alphabet are

Like fat men pushing into us.

We squeeze the girth of the world
And push it out.

We squeeze in the girth of our language
Slowly squeezing it out
With the night of the elephant.

The large grey elephant crusted over with melted star.
Here we stand at the feet of the specialized elephant.
Its translucent spine echoing out all we've ever known of death.

MONSTERS

This is a world where there are monsters

There are monsters everywhere, raccoons and skunks

There are possums outside, there are monsters in my bed.

There is one monster. He is my little one.

I talk to my little monster.

I give my little monster some bacon but that does not satisfy him.

I tell him, sssh sssh, don't growl little monster!

And he growls, oh boy does he growl!

And he wants something from me,

He wants my soul.

And finally giving in, I give him my gleaming soul

And as he eats my gleaming soul, I am one with him

And stare out his eyepits and I see nothing but white

And then I see nothing but fog and the white I had seen before was
    nothing but fog

And there is nothing but fog out the eyes of monsters.

LOVE POEM

The rain whistled.

A taxi brought me to your apartment building
And there I stood.

I had dreamed a dream
Of us in a bedroom.
The light shining upon us in white sheets.

You were singing me a song of your sailing days
And in the dream
I reached deep in you and pulled out a cardinal
Which in bright red
Flew out the window.

Sometimes when we talk
On the phone, I think to myself
That the deep perfect of your soul
Is what draws me to you.
But still what soul is perfect?
All souls are misshapen and off-colored.
Morning comes within a soul
And makes it obey another law
In which all souls are snowflakes.

Once at a funeral, a man had died
And with the prayers said, his soul flew up in a hurry
Like it had been let out of something awful.
It was strangely colored, that soul.
And it was a funny shape and a funny temperature.
As it blew away, all of us looking felt the cold.

I've had a million friends
Lived a lot of different kinds of lives
Said "Oh how's that one?" to a many different kinds of people
I've ridden on the busway with my new friend and then
Found out that I see an old friend
I've talked on the phone to a lot of different people
I've said hello to lots of people and I didn't know their names
I've written letters to friends and mailed them
In the clear light of day, the sun beating on the mailbox
I don't care much for things like that, like friends
I care deeply and when being in love
The sheets upon my face coat over with regret.
Such a wondrous regret! You couldn't even imagine
The ice-sheets on my face, the red flowers of numbers.
The red flower blooming out on the vine
By the stone house where I walk
Humming to myself
See the way the flowers burst out like birds
That's the kind of thing I value

There is a music box playing inside here
And on the wall are tiles by children, painted one day in their art class
See, world, there is art in everything!
You are not so fond of art, you know
The dead woman here thinks she's in Italy
It is Italy inside here, with this ancient music playing.
The dead, plump rat is on the ground.
Uninteresting and blasé, still, it is strange to see a dead, plump rat.
If I were Camus, I would say there is a plague.
Both the dead woman and the rat, as one might say, have slipped
On the cake of the soap of the air.
Now I am sitting by the music box player
Now two women are talking and
Their matching gloves are switched between them.
There is a woman here with a tiny baby
She puts shoes on the baby and talks to it like
A little brown bird, with its red beating breast.
She is old
I wonder if I will be that old when I have a baby
Maybe I will never have a baby
No, that can't be true, out my womb
The tiny babies of the universe will explode.
Outside the station, I dream and act as if I
Am a Harvard student and everyone around me is impressed!
There is a rat inside the T-station who is dead, and plump

Inside my heart, there is a rat who

Eats soap and feeds her babies cakes of soap.

In the dead lady, a rat eats its way out of her.

In the stars, a rat eats noxious gases and then the sun.

The constellations all form in the shapes of rats

And the world from above is blue and brown and slightly sweet smelling.

And inside God, the world of the heart rots and blooms.

This thing started some time ago
O go
O yellow bell
That hangs in my room
You are so low to me
That I feel your soft petals on me
O leave yellow bell
You aren't so pretty to me anymore
The night you fell upon yourself
While all the others watched you
And your yellow petticoats spilled around you
O you weren't so pretty then
Nor were you so wise
You are a machine
And beneath your yellow dress
Is a machine heart
That clicks like an old radio
O hook me up yellow bell
I have always had a weakness
For your kind of love
So precious and dear
So delicate your fingers
As you play me the piano
And grunt in the morning
Things I should remember

If I really loved you
Well I do love you!
Love me too
My heart is so dear to me
I could have been someone
With this throbbing thing
Spilling its red dress everywhere
Making people laugh
I could have made them cry

Friend your body is like the sun and moon put together.

I know that seems strangely sexual,

But there are many forms of grand love that are not sexual.

My friend, the Taurus, has held me down and kissed me many times

And I can't even record to you the things that that awakened.

I think I would like to be dominated in some kind of sadomasochistic way,

But then a man once dominated me with his

Big Buddha-like body and I didn't like that either.

There are people that think my dog should wear a muzzle because
    she growls.

I think their dogs should be put on leashes.

My lover thinks my dog is proof I would be a poor mother.

My lover's thighs only stars, I reach across them into motherhood.

On the tarot card *The Lovers* you my friend read my fortune

And my fortune is dark with unluck.

There is a point zero in which all the death-violets clot into one.

The prophets say we are not one as humans, we are beyond one.

Let me tell you, I am beyond wind.

And the sum of me is as bright as the wind in the morning.

I live too in a bad neighborhood on the other side of town,

Although it is not certainly the sum of all bad neighborhoods, it is bad
    there in my house.

In the middle of the night I wake and I am cold all over.

And in my veins there is ice

And my heart is the warm tap water encased in a block of ice.
And my runny warm heart runs all over him
Who is lying there and my spirit seeps out like a lonely river.
One time we sat at dinner with nothing to say to each other
And before us the great dinner plates of unhappiness
And the sun set on us then and never believed in us again.

LOVE POEM TO MATT AND GRAPES

Grape, grape

A whole world of grapes.

Like a small business

The grape machine is the bustling condition of progress.

It is in progress and growth

That man must marry the heart to Florida.

In Florida, Matt, the grapes grow large and big.

Not in Florida too, my heart is a whirlpool.

From the source of the heart

Is the root that grows thick and purple

And up to my throat it is the yellowbird that sings

She is eating a grape, one dainty leg upon the moon

She is eating the grapes of the world and the fox

He is red too and he is pulling the moon down.

And once he pulls it down, he puts it right back up again.

There are glass animals too, but they do not pull the moon down.

Their hooves and mouths are glass, they do not touch the moon.

YOUR HEART

If you do have a heart
Well then it is very hard for me to see it.
And my heart is bursting forth
Like a bursting flower
Or as a melon, as my friend called it.

My friend's heart is perfume.
I eat her heart with care.

I eat the world lovingly, too.
But you!

Your heart is pity and has no edge
To behold it fully.

And your heart I place on platters.
(It multiplies!)
And your heart I dine on with my children.
And we laugh at you, your little scowl
Is no mark for the great urgency of this world.

WAITING FOR THE DARK,
WAITING FOR THE LIGHT

In the corner sky we built a birdhouse
In it were birds (I hate them)
So I took a picture of Charles
And put it with them
Charles I thought would help
With his sombre walk he was everything else
The red sky was fake fans
The fans were flesh
In the fleshy fans I stood and thought of Charles
Charles was me and I was love
The birds, however, were parts of language
I hate language and yes, I hate you
I hate me and everything else, but I do not hate Charles
He cannot say what he doesn't want to
He takes pictures of girls and he records them, the girls
And on the street he records more
And I follow, I am good at following
And I follow close cause I hate you
And the birds I do not follow them
But one day I jumped and landed on
The grass and thought of them, all blue and snowy
And I thought of Charles, his mouth a sombre white
And the birdhouse I built
From scratch with no tools whatsoever

And the long walk up the morn
With the sun displaying its light as a sorrowful tune
And the sun, heating up my back and neck
And my skin and everything else, slowly dying
And the birds' static cries heard in the distance
And the trees, painted flat and stony white.

What is this journey
That leaves me
And finds me
On the dirt road
With my bloody mouth

And the other wolf
O his mouth aches in mine
O his mouth
Opens in red ribbons
And red windows

O the red room of his mouth
That I am sleeping so soundly in

Art cannot be without love.

There are no paintings done out of hunger.

That is longing you are thinking of, not hunger.

In you, I am sitting alone on a frighteningly sunny day.

The yellow sun rays making even my fingernails seem blue.

My ankles are completely shaven.

I am like some kind of freak,

Except now, you see, love is on my side.

I am eating tropical jelly beans and drinking coffee.

I have just gotten satsuma body wash and

Elderflower eye gel and orange essence facial cleanser.

Later I will take a bath in bergamots

And the bathroom will fill with moonsun.

The clear milky light will flood on me.

Completely bloodless, I in the white tub, surrounded with greenish fruits,

Will be almost not breathing.

The great event which is beauty

Can only happen when one is full.

You to me are like leaves on candy.

All of a sudden the candy is growing

And from the candy, blue flowers and leaves grow.

Made entirely of sugar,

Their grainy pores give food to the soul.

AFTER THE APOCALYPSE

THERE IS ONLY THE APOCALYPSE

The sun came streaming in
Melting the things in the room
The papers crumbled into a black heap
The furniture crawled and then disappeared

The fire in the sun is a person
He and I once ate lunch
On the moon we sat with a blanket and a picnic basket
He said the world before us is nothing compared

To the fire in his heart and the fire in God
That makes the whole world
Thump in a beating music, heartbeats and mountains
That makes the bluebird in the tree

Swoop down to a small river
And wet his silky blue body.
A red worm in his mouth
And the sun a yellow light on his back.

IN ORDER TO PENETRATE CHARACTER
ONE MUST HAVE GREAT PIETY

There have been times love has made my human
Instincts into animal ones.
Once in a dark lit bar, my love said my poems were shit
And I, in the light of the candles,
Pushed a sword into myself and fell over a cliff
Into a neverending ocean.
Once a man 5 years my younger
Loved me and then gave me up.
I raged around him like a bear.
I once cheated on a new boyfriend with an old boyfriend.
I cheated on an old boyfriend with a new one.
Love has the ability to make the world kind,
The specifics of one man always blends into another
And turns back into my mother's kisses on my cheek.
It is I who loves, but it is in turn
The world that loves me back. The world loves
And I love back, the specifics of it
Once in tune. Once we kissed and I was
Mesmerized by the blondness of his cheek
With the light on it and the sweet smell of the earth.
But still the light on the cheek is the desert lizards
Who will eat us in the afterworld and in the light of the moon
There is the exhaust of love falling over everything.

BOOBS ARE REAL

They stole my tires
They knocked down my house
They killed my father
They cut off my fingers
And I thought, "And I did like those fingers."

They pierced my eyelids. They scalped my brain.
They ran their sweaty fingers down my sweaty back.
They played me music but it wasn't music.
They loved me and then they didn't.
Somewhere in there I grew these enormous boobs.
At some point what they took away
Was given back
In the form of boobs.
What they took from me
They gave back
Just like, as Lydia Davis says,
When a limit has been reached
What is real but does not help
Is lost forever and replaced by the unreal.
The difference is: these boobs are real.

I WILL EXPLAIN MY SCHEME

I had almost forgotten I was a poet
But I am a poet!
It was Jason's birthday today
He probably thought I had forgotten him
I hadn't.
The sun I had not forgotten.
Blood?
Nope.
And music too and pretty things
Well, I hoped I had forgotten those.
The morning rose with such urgency
I wanted to forget urgency
And couldn't.

Jesus, whatever they call you
I will always be pro-love.

Whatever folds open in the formal sky
It will be I
That lands the rushing straight to its feet
And on me, rushing things
And things folding upon each other.
And the things that fold upon each other
Those things will be my voice.

I WAS ONCE VERY SMART

When you said I was smart, you probably meant
I was a philosopher.

Stopping the car and thinking, too, does not necessarily
Mean you're smart, but it probably does.

Being smart means your mind has
Been whipped by the large whisk of God.

Now your brain sits on your head
And you can see most things.

The injustices themselves are obvious.
For instance, it is tears that drench your face.

It is animal jaw that is shot down and eaten.
It is child that is killed, too and wept.

When the stars shoot out
It is my heart that listens

The sun like a fog
And all that is real like a bitter silence.

The face of the universe, wet and sucking in air.

YOU AIN'T GONNA GET GLORY
IF THAT'S WHAT YOU CAME HERE FOR

If no one wants to make a home with me
Then I will make a home with myself
And wait for someone
To plant the flowers outside my window
And make me pudding
While I write poems
And the fragile parts of me
Will be senseless.
Conceptual art is dead.
Language poetry, you know how I feel.
Kenneth Koch, you are dead, too.
All the others are not the ones to follow.
Follow me, I know everything.
Follow me
Art is not sense broken up into line
You with your lover there, you are not the birdhouse
The children coming from your womb
Are not longing made into flesh
You are not flesh, too
And flesh is not modern
It is old Mary on her throne
Sweetly coughing up angels

From a deep and sudden throat and the blueness of her dress is real
And her flaming heart with stakes in it feels a real and sudden pain
From a place we cannot imagine
And is felt everywhere, the blood running through it,
Sugary sweet there, and soft.

Someone I had thought was my husband
Wasn't my husband and I wasn't in love with him and I wasn't in love
    with anyone.

And the soles of my feet were bloodied
And my back was bloodied and my mother poured blood all over me

And my mouth was brimming with blood
And my skin hurt from all the bleeding and my brain hurt
Brimming to its edges with blood and the blood in me was cold.

That was the worst part. And the blood pouring all over my face was
    ice cold.
And there was nothing warm anywhere.

And outside was cold and rotting and the trees were rotting with a
    great disease.

And the trees were rotting and to my side, my friend was having a baby.
And she handed me the baby and I kissed its bleeding head.

And we sang songs together and being each other
We kissed each other lovingly for the very first time.
And the world opened up and a great light shone.

And on a sepulcher a bloodied stranger motioned to my right
And to my right was nothing and to this day, I grasp at nothing.

But being a bloodied stranger, too, I took
The stranger in my mouth and held him there for a very long time.

And when time expired, we both melted and the
Sun lit on the heavens both bullish and cold.

And the sun lit on the heavens and iced the world
An icy blue and the icy blue expanded itself

And now, my child, you see this in front of you is only morning.

Thank you to my parents, Carole and Herbert Lasky, and to my family, friends, and teachers for their immeasurable love and support. A special thank you goes to Joshua Beckman. Without his brilliant editorial work and continued belief in these poems, this book would have not been possible.

Thank you to the following journals, where some of the poems were originally published: *6×6*, *Boston Review*, *Castagraf*, *Crowd*, *Drill Magazine*, *Filter*, *jubilat*, *Phoebe*, *String of Small Machines*, and *Word For/Word*. Thank you to the editors of the following presses for originally publishing some of these poems in chapbooks: *The Hatmaker's Wife* (Braincase Press, 2006), *Art* (H_NGM_N B__KS, 2005), and *Alphabets and Portraits* (Anchorite Press, 2004).